Your Twelve Step Journey:

A Journey and a Guide

Barbara Niemeyer

Third Edition

Serenity Prayer

By

Reinhold Niebuhr

God, grant me the serenity

To accept the things I cannot change

Courage to change the things I can

And the wisdom to know the difference.

~Amen~

The 12 Steps

Step 1. We admitted we were powerless over alcohol, that our lives had become unmanageable.

Step 2. Came to believe that a Power greater than ourselves could restore us to sanity.

Step 3. Made a decision to turn our will and our lives over to the care of God as we understood Him.

Step 4. Made a searching and fearless moral inventory of ourselves.

Step 5. Admitted to God, to ourselves, and to another human being the exact nature of our wrongs.

Step 6. Were entirely ready to have God remove all these defects of character.

Step 7. Humbly asked Him to remove our shortcomings
.

Step 8. Made a list of all persons we had harmed, and became willing to make amends to them all.

Step 9. Made direct amends to such people wherever possible, except when to do so would injure them or others.

Step 10. Continued to take personal inventory and when we were wrong promptly admitted it.

Step 11. Sought through prayer and meditation to improve our conscious contact with God as we understood Him, praying only for knowledge of His will for us and the power to carry that out.

Step 12. Having had a spiritual awakening as the result of these steps, we tried to carry this message to others, and to practice these principles in all our affairs.

Forward

After attending a few meetings of Al-Anon, I realized that my recovery and the program centered upon working the twelve steps. Yet, there was no one I was drawn to ask to be my sponsor in my small local group. After several months and a few attempts with a temporary sponsor, I began to work the steps on my own. This wasn't my first rodeo.

Conventional wisdom will encourage you to work the twelve steps with a sponsor. A newcomer to the program will find many potential pitfalls when there is not a sponsor to provide insights and guidance. In fact, I later re-worked those steps with a veteran sponsor who brought a deeper level of understanding and a transformation of my being. Yet, everyone must begin somewhere. Every journey begins with a single step.

Barbara brought this project to me as a workbook for sponsors to use as a handbook for their new sponsees. Using a journal provides a great advantage in the path to recovery. You can see progress throughout the twelve step journey. The materials are organized to reflect on the insights of the prior step. When you stall out on a step, you can go back to the beginning and gain new clarity to your work on yourself.

Drawing on my past experience in sponsoring others, I asked Barbara to broaden her perspective of this workbook to include those of us who need to begin the journey on our own. As the group always reminded me, "We work the program in our own way."

This book was designed to be used by addicts and those that love them. Many recovering addicts begin Alanon at some point to learn recovery from a different perspective. Those who do are called double winners.

I hope you find this project of value in working your own path to serenity. You're worth it.

Gayle Clayton MA

Author, *Seeking Higher Power*

What brought you here?

This is a question that I am often asked in my online and face to face groups. Occasionally, I tell my story. I'm no longer nervous about that. Everyone who comes to a meeting has a similar story. We're all there for the same reasons.

Anonymity is the foundation that provides a safe space to share the truth. You don't have to give your last name or share unless you want to. Our secrets have power over us and telling the truth can be such a relief.

Whenever I get asked to share with a newcomer, I trust that my Higher Power will give me the words that the newcomer needs to hear. I have found that a big part of working the steps is sharing my experience, strength and hope with another.

In the end, what brought us here is also an inspiration for transforming our lives.

Please stop and reflect what brought you to this point in your life.

____

____

____

____

____

____

____

____

____

The truth will set you free,

but first it might tick you off.

Step 1

We admitted we were powerless over alcohol, that our lives had become unmanageable.

I walked into my first 12 step meeting lost, upset and looking for help. I knew something had to change. My main thought was to get help for the alcoholic/addict in my life. Little did I know that I was taking the first step in changing me.

Slowly the people in the program shifted my focus. I wasn't a victim. Addiction is a disease. So whether an addict or a person loving one, the three C's are at the core of understanding. I didn't Cause this disease, I certainly couldn't Cure it and I know that the actions of people, places and things are out of my Control. These are the three "C's". A fourth "C" is, "how have I Contributed to the problem?"

The process is not that different for addicts and those who love them. When addicts reach bottom, frequently the consequences of their actions are more dire and perhaps more urgent to address. However, at bottom, there is only one direction to go: start climbing up.

Every journey begins with a single step. By the time people seek help, step one feels like relief. Life has become chaotic, out of control, and hopeless. However, there is always hope. Breathe deeply-realize that you are not alone in these situations. Many others share your story and some have completed the journey you are about to begin.

As I worked this step I saw just how unmanageable my life had become. One of the tools that I learned to use is detachment. When I detach I realize that the person I love is separate from the disease of alcoholism and addiction. I began to understand that they suffer from a disease as much as a person with diabetes or cancer suffers. I still love them even though they have this disease. When I learned detachment I became better able to distance myself emotionally from the effects of alcoholism and addiction.

Working this step with addicts is often a bit harder. If in a rehab, they are sheltered from the consequences that their addiction causes. Yet, treatment is no high class camp; it is an intense development of a normal schedule with people holding you accountable for your actions and insights into what addiction is. Yet many people get sober without entering a rehab center and some without using the twelve steps. (In Al-anon circles, these people are often called "dry drunks" since they still exhibit addict behavior without using.) Yet, the twelve steps are about changing thought patterns and behavior. To begin step one is to recognize the denial of the effects of the drug of choice and its consequences.

Addiction is a family disease. Every addict affects at least 15 people in their sphere of influence. Learning how to control myself and my reactions to events caused by others became a main concern. There were decisions to make. What could I control? What did I want to control? As a mother, my children's education is very important to me. I want them to learn as much as they can. But I cannot do the work for them. My sixth grader is going to have to write that paper himself. After all it is his grade, not mine. Standing back and letting others excel and/or fail and manage their own lives was one of the lessons Step 1 taught me.

Recovery means taking care of your-self in healthy ways. Many use as self-medication. When addicts quit using, reality raises its ugly head to reveal underlying insecurities, issues, rebellion, and even anger. Luckily, people can resolve issues, learn different management or coping skills, and create healthy boundaries in their lives.

One of the benefits I discovered in letting others manage their own lives came when I found myself with a lot of free time on my hands. I began to take a look at areas of my life that needed attention. I needed to get healthy, physically and emotionally. I began to take a close look at what I was doing to myself as a result of my unmanageable life. Eat right, quit smoking, exercise, go to my meetings, talk to my therapist and/or my sponsor. Work on me for a change instead of everyone else. All of this came as a result of working Step 1. This step gave me hope and an eagerness to work the rest of the twelve steps.

Begin this process with gentleness with yourself. Let go of your judgment. It is what it is. Here are some questions to help you with working Step 1. Answer the ones that are applicable to you. Do yourself a favor and write the answers down even if you do not feel comfortable in writing in this book. You don't have to use complete sentences. Jot down key words or phrases for your own understanding.

Writing makes the process more real. When you come back later to look at where you were, you will be amazed by your progress.

If you have a sponsor or can share with a person who has successfully completed 12 step work, review your answers or ask questions before moving on to step 2.

Questions:

Define the word powerless. ______________________________________

____

Give some examples of powerlessness in your life.

____

____

____

____

____

How has drinking/drugging or dealing with an addict affected your life?

____

____

____

____

Why are you working a 12 step program?

____

____

____

Why should you continue working in a 12 step program?

____

____

____

Every journey begins with a single step.

You can do this.

Who and what can you control in your life?

_____

_____

_____

_____

_____

What have you learned about the 3 C's?

_____

_____

_____

_____

_____

_____

_____

_____

What did you do to cause the problem?

_____

_____

How can you cure this problem?

_____

_____

Let go or be dragged.

What have you done to try to control this problem?

How has drinking/drugging or dealing with the addict caused problems in your professional life?

Detachment: Separation of self from events, words, people, and things that are outside our realm of control through the use of healthy boundaries.

How did/do you contribute to the problem?

____

____

____

____

____

____

How might (you let) the alcoholic/addict take the consequences for their own behavior?

____

____

____

____

____

Can you give some examples of your use of detachment?

____

____

____

____

____

____

____

____

Keep coming back.

How are you making your life more manageable?

____

____

____

____

____

____

____

Have you truly admitted that you are powerless over alcohol, over alcoholism, over the alcoholic, and over every one, except yourself?

____

Think of ways of how you are working this step.

____

____

____

____

____

____

____

____

____

____

____

I am powerless over ____________.

What topics of discussion or questions have you had in working this step?

Step 2

Came to believe that a Power greater than ourselves could restore us to sanity.

I approached this step with the hope that there is something out there that could help-whether it be the group, God or my own self-defined Higher Power. The hope and realization that things can get better is key to my recovery.

For me, this step marked the beginning of the discovery of whom or what is a Higher Power. I began to look at my own concepts of spirituality, religion and even God. I was coming to believe that the fellowship of the group, my Higher Power or something outside of myself could restore me to sanity. I was becoming willing to accept the help of my Higher Power.

When I was growing up God and/or religion was not a part of my life. I knew there was something out there, but I did not know what. I didn't question why my family did not go to church. It was just the way it was. When I married, my spouse was disillusioned by his own religious upbringing so going to church was not in the equation.

It wasn't until I discovered my 12 step group that I even began to question my own beliefs. Was there really something out there that could restore me to sanity? And if so what was it? Who was it? And why did it care about me?

I knew next to nothing about God or the Bible, but my 12 step group made it easy for me to ask questions and point out several paths to follow in finding my way to the answers I sought. I discovered that this step nor this program was about religion. It did not matter who I found as my Higher Power. What was important was for me to realize I could not do this program without help.

Realize that this step is not about defining who/what god or a higher power is. Realize that there is something that is more than you. After all, if you were in charge of the world, would you be in this place of chaos? The second part of the step is also important. There is hope that you can be restored to sanity. Few people in this world are an island.

Questions:

Describe your Higher Power.

____

____

____

____

____

____

How has your concept of Higher Power changed through the years?

____

____

____

____

____

____

What is your process of "Coming to Believe"?

____

____

____

____

____

____

Describe some of the insanity in your life:

____

____

____

____

____

____

What inspires you to stay sober or to find serenity?

____

____

____

____

____

____

How do you use the Serenity Prayer?

____

____

____

____

____

____

____

____

Insanity is doing the same things over and over and expecting different results.

Describe where you go to find serenity.

____

____

____

____

____

____

What things can you not change?

____

____

____

____

____

____

How have you found the courage in your life to make changes?

____

____

____

____

____

____

God grant me the Serenity to accept the things I cannot change...

Courage to change the things I can

and Wisdom to know the difference...

What is the difference between hope and expectations?

Do you believe in miracles? Why or why not?

Can you describe any miracles that have occurred in your life recently?

Miracles Happen.

Why do you believe that a Power greater than yourself can restore you to sanity?

____

____

____

____

____

____

What are you feeling while you are working Step 2?

____

____

____

____

____

____

What are some of the topics of discussion your sponsor/trusted friend and you have had in working this step?

____

____

____

____

____

When I got busy,

I got better.

Step 3

Made a decision to turn our will and our lives over to the care of God as we understood Him.

Step 3 often is a stumbling block. For many of us it may begin with the word God. Yet as I began my search for a higher power greater than myself, I substituted Higher Power (HP) for the word God. The freedom of my own understanding gave me liberation in this step. Working the twelve steps does not have to be done under a religious tradition.

After jumping that hurdle which may have been part of my own denial of my state, I immediately stopped short when asked to turn over my will. Many of us have fought to have our own way for a long time. Yet, when we look at where we are right now, how well have we managed our own lives? How well have we kept the commitments we made? Are we happy?

There may be a better way. There are multiple layers of understanding in Step 3. In working toward a relationship with a higher power, perhaps we are looking for a good coach, a benevolent figure, or an understanding guide. Higher power can be defined in your own terms instead of what you may have been taught. Explore your own beliefs and understanding.

It is good to know that while I am responsible for my own foot-work, my higher power is there to guide me on my path. Listening to his will and letting go of mine is key. The moment I discovered I had a choice was very freeing. Doing things the same way over and over again has not worked. Forcing situations and people to do as "I" will is not working. It is "God's" will that must be listened to.

Letting go of the outcomes of the situations in my life is the way to serenity. My life will be a lot happier if I let go of the expectations I have of others and just focus on myself. Letting my family members make their own mistakes and suffer their own consequences was hard. But they needed to experience life also. Their lives are not mine to live. They have their own higher power to discover.

Sometimes it takes a while to figure out what God's will really is. I was wrestling with a decision I was trying to make, calling my sponsor, a few members of my group and a couple of friends. No one was available. I was getting more anxious by the minute. But then at a stop light, I called out, expressing my frustration and all of a sudden I felt like someone had turned the switch on in my head. I didn't need to hash over my decisions and reasons with the world, I needed to talk directly to the one person this decision affected.

Once I realized this, I gained the confidence and determination to go and make my decision known. I felt a sense of release when finished and realized that the whole process was my Higher Power (HP) making his will known to me and next time if I pay a bit more attention, I may not have to go through all the stress I was creating for myself.

While working this step, I found myself looking for signs of God's will all over the place. It is amazing how he lets us know whether it is the right or wrong thing to do. A clue may be in a song I hear, or a billboard I pass on the freeway or even a chance remark by a coworker.

If I am going through a particularly hard time, it may be HP's way of saying there is a lesson to be learned and if I don't get it the first time, I may have to keeping working away at it until I get it right. But that is okay, because I am where I need to be-right now.

There is a higher power.

I'm not it.

Questions:

What good decisions have you been making lately?

____

____

____

____

____

____

In what ways does your will and God's will coincide?

____

____

____

____

____

____

Is there anyone or anything that you trust?

____

____

____

____

____

____

Is my way working?

How does “Let Go and Let God” work in your life?

____

____

____

____

____

____

How do you feel about giving up control of your life and placing it in your Higher Power’s hands?

____

____

____

____

____

____

What do you do when others do not agree with your decisions?

____

____

____

____

____

Expand the possible.

How much energy to you expend in resisting making changes in your life?

Have you started to recognize the signs that you are about to relapse? What do you do about it?

What is your process for giving your will over to your Higher Power?

What are your triggers

that take you back to your old way of life?

Who made decisions for you while you were using? How about now? While you are in recovery?

____

____

____

____

____

____

Describe any moments that are "Happy, Joyous and Free" since you have started working this progam?

____

____

____

____

____

____

____

How do you use the slogan “One day at a time”?

____

____

____

____

____

WORK IN PROGRESS

What happens when your plans for the day become disrupted?

How do you react when you discover you are not right?

How do you plan to live your life once you turn your life over to your Higher Power?

You can start your day over at any time.

Have you truly made a decision to turn your life and will over to the care of your Higher Power? Give some examples of how you are working step 3 in order to do so.

What are some of the topics of discussion that your sponsor/trusted friend and you have had in working this step? What questions do you have?

The ABC'S

of

Gratitude

One of the tools I use when I am down or depressed is making a gratitude list. Most of us have something to be thankful for. I know I do. It can be for the roof over my head, that it is not raining today or that I got to sit down for fifteen minutes and talk to a friend.

When I wake up every morning I try to think of the three top things I am grateful for in my life. As I go throughout the day, I add to the list. Usually I am surprised by how long it is by bedtime.

Play a game with a friend or a group by taking turns listing everything you are grateful for by using the alphabet. For example…A=Attitude (I am a lot more positive these days) B=Blessed (I am blessed to have found so many friends in this program) and on until you finish up with the letter Z.

Next go back and do the same with your resentments.

Which was harder to do? Why do you think that is?

Alphabet Gratitude List

A	**B**
C	**D**
E	**F**
G	**H**
I	**J**
K	**L**
M	**N**
O	**P**
Q	**R**
S	**T**
U	**V**
W	**X**
Y	**Z**

Resentments are like stray cats.

If you don’t feed them, they go away.

Alphabet Resentment List

A	**B**
C	**D**
E	**F**
G	**H**
I	**J**
K	**L**
M	**N**
O	**P**
Q	**R**
S	**T**
U	**V**
W	**X**
Y	**Z**

Step 4

Made a searching and fearless moral inventory of ourselves.

Step 4 was for me my most feared step. Everybody had talked of their personal inventory and the turmoil it stirred up.With so little self-esteem, it hardly seemed like the time to uncover all my defects. Fortunately a friend reminded me it was also a time to inventory my assets as well.

This was an emotional time in my life. Things popped up into my awareness unexpectedly. I found that it was best to deal with these things as they came up and not bury them. Memories, good and bad surfaced. Journaling helped keep things in perspective. When I shared these things with my sponsor, I was able to spot trends and patterns of behavior. Sometimes my sponsor pointed them out to me if I was not seeing what was in front of my face.

Being honest and willing helped get me through it. This is not a step to be rushed through. I gave myself a goal with a deadline. While it took me two months to finish this step, others work it faster or slower. It's not a race. You work at your own pace. I had a lot going on at the time, but I made sure that I sat down every day and did something. I learned so much about myself. And one of the funny things is, some of the things I learned, others had known for a while.

I was fortunate that I could make this step with a sponsor. She helped me keep things in perspective and didn't let me be too hard on myself. In my inventory I discovered that I had assets as well as defects. It was during this step that I become aware of the items in my inventory. I acknowledged them and realized that acting upon this list would come later.

There were times during the process that I would throw my notebook up against the wall in frustration. I couldn't do this, I didn't want to do this, it was too hard. Oh the excuses that ran through my head. Then it came to me that what I was doing (throwing a hissy fit) right then should be on the list of character defects. I was able to laugh at my behavior, find it on the list and be done with it.

One of the tricks I used to complete my 4th step was for every character defect I found, I had to find two character assets. This helped keep me from beating myself up and come to the realization that I was truly was a good person. Not perfect but then again, no one is.

Listing of Character Defects:

Not all of these character defects may apply. But for those that do, think about them, and decide where they fit in your life. You may not see a defect in yourself, but others may and this might be a good time to ask questions about it. Circle those you think you may have. Add ones that aren't listed.

Aloofness...Anger....Apathy...Argumentative...Arrogance...Attention-seeking

Bitter...Bossy...Braggart

Careless...Cold hearted...Complainer...Compulsive...Critical

Deceitful...Defensiveness...Denial...Dependent...Depression...Detached

Dishonesty...Disorganized...Distant...Distrustful...Dominating...Dramatic

Egocentric...Enviousness...Evasiveness

Fear...Flightiness...Forgetfulness

Gluttony...Gossiping...Greed...Guilty Conscience

Hate...Headstrong...Hostile...Humorless

Immature...Impatience...Impulsive...Inconsistent...Indecisive

Indulgent...Inhibited...Insecure...Insensitive...Intolerant...Irritable

Isolation

Jealousy...Laziness...Lying...Manipulative...Materialism...Negative Thinking

Neglect...Obsessed...Opinionated...Over-cautious...Overly-emotional

Passivity...Perfectionism...Pessimism...Preoccupation...Pride... Procrastination

Prudish...Quarrelsome...Rageful...Rebellious...Reckless...Resentful

Rudeness...Rueful...Sarcasm...Secretive...Self-centered...Self-condemnation

Self-doubting...Self-hating...Self-importance...Selfishness...Self-justification

Self-pity...Self-seeking...Short-tempered...Shyness...Snobbery...Stinginess

Stubbornness...Submissive...Superficial...Thin-skinned ...Thoughtless ...Tight

Timid...Uncritical...Undependable...Undisciplined...Unemotional... Unfriendly

Unrealistic...Unromantic...Unscrupulous...Unstable...Vague...Vanity...

Vindictive

Vulgar...White-knuckled...Withdrawn...Workaholic

Character Assets

Not all of these assets may apply. But for those that do, think about them, and decide where they fit in your life. You may not see the asset in yourself but others may and this might be a good time to ask questions about it.

Accepting...Agreeable...Analytical...Approving...Assertive...Attention-giving...Attentive…Bold...

Careful...Cautious...Cheerful...Concerned...Confident...Considerate...

Content…Controlled...Cooperative..Decisive.. Dependable. .Disciplined...Extroverted

Flexible...Forgiving...Free...Friendly...Generous...Gentle...Good Listener

Giving...Guiltfree...Helpful..Honest...Humble….Industrious...Involved

Kind…Lawful...Loving...Moderate...Modest...Nice...Open...Open-minded...Optimistic…Organized

Outgoing...Patient...Peaceful...Permissive...Persistent...Playful…

Polite…Rational...Realistic...Relaxed..Reliable...Romantic...Selfless...

Self-liking...Self-sufficient Sensitive...Serene...Sociable...Social. ..Specific...Spiritual...Steady...Straightforward

Thoughtful...Tolerant...Trusting...Unassuming...Venturous...Warm...

Witty

If you keep doing what you're doing

you'll keep getting what you're getting.

Questions:

How has working this step influenced your various relationships? IE: work, immediate and extended families, partner/spouse?

What causes you to be fearful?

Do you find yourself thinking before reacting? Can you think of any examples of this?

Spot it? Got it.

Which pattern of behavior bothers you the most?

____

____

____

____

What do you like about yourself? What do others like about you?

____

____

____

____

Do you have problems admitting where you are at fault?

____

____

____

____

How is your self-image now as compared to what it was before you started working the steps?

____

____

____

____

There are two emotions: Love and Fear.

The first is our natural inheritance,

and the other our minds manufacture.

Do you have difficulties with trust and /or making commitments with a significant other?

What memories do you have that are still painful?

Do you find it difficult to be intimate with your spouse/partner?

Are your needs often overlooked in your effort to please your spouse/partner in bed?

I ain't what I oughta be

I ain't what I wanta be

I ain't what I'm gonna be

but I ain't what I usta be

How well do you take compliments? Why?

What is your opinion of the quality of your sex life?

How do you use sex as a means to control others in your life?

How important is sex in your relationship with your spouse/partner?

Who you see here;

what you hear here;

when you leave here;

let it stay here.

What are your feelings in completing this step, do you truly believe you have made a searching and fearless moral inventory of yourself? What assets surprised you the most? What defects?

Step 5

Admitted to God, to ourselves, and to another human being the exact nature of our wrongs.

Step 5 required that I trust my higher power and another person. Trust is a huge issue for me. However, I remembered that my Higher Power and my sponsor both loved me the way I was. That helped immensely. I was surprised to find out that my story had similarities to my sponsor's story.

My purpose in taking this step was to admit my wrongs. Saying things aloud was quite different than just writing these items. Sharing these intimate flaws brought up feelings of inadequacy, of not being loved, of not doing everything perfectly, and feeling that I was not good enough. The support of peers undergoing the same process helped me summon my courage.

I was pleasantly surprised when I was finished with my self-revelations that I was not judged. Both my sponsor and Higher Power heard me with love and compassion.

Some people take the fifth step all at once; others take it little by little. There is no wrong way to do step five. I sat down with my sponsor and finished it in an afternoon. The feeling of relief that occurred when I realized steps four and five were done was immense. Like a big weight off my shoulders. It can be scary baring your soul to another person. But when I accepted the love and support that was shown to me from my sponsor and Higher Power, it was not as daunting.

Complete honesty was the outcome for me in step 5. I do not think I had ever been completely honest with myself, Higher Power or another person until I worked this step. What was the point of lying or hiding the truth from anyone? If I wasn't completely honest I might as well have just gone back to step 1 and began again. My ears were buzzing and my chest hurt as I admitted to God and my sponsor my wrongs. It was tough to get it all out, but I did and I felt so much better for doing so.

A couple of days after it was over, I had some fleeting thoughts as to what my sponsor would think of me after hearing all of my dirt. But I realized that here was one person who knew me better than I knew myself. Here was someone who understood and loved me anyway.

Questions:

Are you afraid to admit things to your Higher Power? If so, what sort of things do you not want to talk to your Higher Power about?

What does awareness have to do in the process of admitting your wrongs to yourself?

What will it take to trust enough to tell another human being the nature of your wrongs?

Honesty is the best policy.

How will faith help you in taking this step?

____

____

____

____

What have you hidden from your Higher Power or the person with whom you are taking step 5?

____

____

____

____

Have you truly admitted to your Higher Power and another person the exact nature of your wrongs?

____

____

What is your plan on getting rid of unhealthy behaviors and courting healthy behaviors?

____

____

____

____

Courage is not the absence of fear,

but the ability to act in spite of it.

What triggers do you have that cause unhealthy behaviors to return? How can you combat them?

What are your expectations about working this step?

What are some examples on how you are working step 5?

How did you feel after completing this step?

Activity

Step 1 was learning all about how truly powerless we are over the alcohol/drug addiction. We may be powerless over the disease, but we do have control over what and how we think and control over our own actions.

Now that you have completed your 4th step it is easier to recognize events that may trigger a relapse. A relapse is not just succumbing to a drink or a drug, it can be a relapse in your thinking and in your behaviors.

My husband came home an hour late from work last night. What did I do? Did I immediately go up to him and start looking for signs that he had been drinking? Did he smell like smoke? Had he been in a bar? Are his eyes red or dilated? Or did I greet him and let him wind down and let him explain why he was late coming home in his own time?

A trigger could be finding some extra money in your pocket, or reacting to the extra work your boss assigned you or even hearing co-workers talk about going out after work to a restaurant or bar. In this activity think or talk about past triggers you have had and come up with some solutions for each one so that you are not caught unawares.

Have a plan on how to deal with your most common triggers. Role play with another person if that will help. For example if a coworker starts talking about a big party they are having this weekend and you are invited, talk to another person about how to go about dealing with this situation. Do you go and hope that you don't drink, do you go with another person to help hold you accountable or do you decline the invitation graciously? Think of your most common triggers and come up with a plan to get past them.

What are some of the topics of discussion have you and your sponsor/trusted friend have had in working step 5?

Step 6

Were entirely ready to have God remove all these defects of character.

I was so miserable that I had to get rid of some of the bad stuff in my life. Change did not come easy. I found out that my Higher Power was willing to help me as long as I was willing to ask. After revealing all to my Higher Power, it came as a relief to know that He would remove my defects.

Some of these defects have been around for a long time. At first it seemed easier to keep them than to give them up. But after taking the 4th and 5th step I realized that my defects no longer served me. In fact they were holding me back in my recovery.

As I prepared for God to remove my defects, I also had to think about some of my assets. What could I do to expand upon these? What assets did I lack that I would like to develop? Talking to my sponsor/trusted friend, helped me to see what I was missing.

Being in control of everything was one of the hardest defects to let go of. I was the one who was always in charge of everything and everyone in my family. I was the "boss". My ex-spouse even had a t-shirt that said "Yes Dear" on it. My whole family knew that if you gave the project to me that it would get done. But as I found out, everyone has their limit. I reached mine and crashed down to earth. I knew that on order to get healthy again, others needed to take back their stuff and let me deal with my own.

When I feel the temptation to take control of something or even find myself in charge, I ask myself is this necessary? Or why am I doing this? Am I afraid the job won't get done to my expectation? What am I afraid of if I let this situation go? I am finding that it is nice to sit back and relax and enjoy myself instead of being all stressed out over something that wasn't mine in the first place.

Let go and let Higher Power.

Questions:

What does "entirely ready" mean to you?

What character defects are you unwilling to let go of?

Do you pray to your Higher Power for willingness?

Which defects at this time are you willing to let your Higher Power have?

Humility is like underwear,

it's necessary but it's indecent if it shows.

Have you been honest in your 4th step inventory?

Do you need to go back and revisit any parts of your 4th step and expand on some of your answers?

Are you truly entirely ready to have your Higher Power remove all your defects of character? Why or why not?

Tomorrow's resentments

are fed by today's expectations.

Give an example of how you are working step 6.

What are some of the topics of discussion have you and your sponsor/trusted friend have had in working this step? Any questions?

Step 7

Humbly asked Him to remove our shortcomings.

If I do not ask for help in removing my shortcomings, how will they be removed? It has already been established that my will alone does not work. Having faith in my Higher Power will make the removal of my shortcomings a lot easier to handle.

I have found many ways to ask Him to remove my shortcomings. I have gotten down on my knees and prayed and experienced immediate relief. Other times I have prayed all day every day and little by little my shortcomings were stripped away. Sometimes it takes a while for me to become ready for some of my defects to be taken from me. I take them back and wrestle around with them before I try again.

This step marks the beginning of a changed attitude about my defects and shortcomings. I am refusing to fall victim to them any longer and I beg my Higher Power to give me the strength to make the change in my life.

I have struggled with fear in all aspects of my life. Fear of stepping outside my comfort zone. Not wanting to try new experiences. Using fear as an excuse to not grow or recover, falling back on the "this is the way it has always been" mentality.

In an effort to remove the fear, I have adopted an attitude of doing things afraid. With my Higher Power's help I have decided that there are only three outcomes that can happen while doing something afraid.

- One, I will decide that it wasn't so bad after all.
- Two, it was scary but HP got me through it and I am stronger for it.
- Three, it was the worst experience of my life and I am never doing that again, but I am proud of myself for trying.

What doesn't kill us makes us stronger.

Questions:

What impact does prayer have in your life?

____

____

____

Is there a difference between a character defect and a shortcoming?

____

____

____

____

What slogans do you use when old behaviors reappear? And how do they help you?

____

____

____

____

What part does willingness play in this step?

____

____

____

____

Let me be willing to be willing.

What character asset are you going to cultivate to replace the shortcoming you are asking your Higher Power to get rid of?

____
____
____
____
____
____

What shortcomings are you afraid to have taken away?

____
____
____
____

How does humility help you understand your Higher Power?

____
____
____
____
____
____
____
____

One Day At a Time

Have you humbly asked your Higher Power to remove all of your shortcomings? Why not?

____

____

____

____

What do you think your life will be like when your character defects are removed?

____

____

____

____

____

What is it in your life that restores your hope?

____

____

____

____

What can you do to make sure these influences stay in your life?

____

____

Dare to hope.

Give an example of how you are working step 7.

What are some of the topics of discussion between you and your sponsor/trusted friend in working step 7?

Step 8

Made a list of all persons we had harmed, and became willing to make amends to them all.

Making amends to other people was not so much for them but for me. How others reacted to my amends was not under my control. I found that it was easier to make amends to some people than it was to others. I had to pray to become willing. It was easier when I felt that I could do it. That it was possible. I had to check my motives. Why did I want to make amends to this person on my list? I needed to look through my 4th step again. Was there a reason I couldn't or wouldn't make amends to someone I had harmed. As I compiled my list, I found myself forgiving some people on my list for harms that I thought were committed against me. As time went on, I became willing to make amends to them as well.

The first people I put on my list were my parents. I had spent years hiding all of the chaos that was my marriage. No one had a clue that my life was surrounded by addictions and the behavior associated with them. Whenever they would call, as far as they were concerned everything was perfectly fine. And if we were visiting, I worked double time to hide any evidence that we were having problems. I wanted that white picket fence image to remain intact.

I can only imagine the shock and hurt that they felt when they saw my life fall apart. And the realization that I did not trust them enough to share with them the struggles I was having. I had too much pride to allow them to help me and I needed to make amends for this.

Gradually I made a list of everyone I had wronged in the past, including me.

Questions:

Who is first on your list and why?

How did you review your Fourth Step to help make your list?

How did asking someone to help make your list change it?

What is your part in the harming of the people on your list?

Don’t give in to Stinkin’ Thinkin!

What is the difference between making amends and apologizing?

What sort of amends can you make to the people on your list?

Why are you willing to make amends?

What prevents you from being willing to make amends?

Live and let live.

Have you made your list of the people you have harmed and became willing to make amends to them all?

Give an example of how you are working step 8.

What are some of the topics of discussion have you and your sponsor/trusted friend have had in working this step?

Step 9

Made direct amends to such people wherever possible, except when to do so would injure them or others.

In order for amends to mean anything to myself or others, my behavior must change. Behavior changes may be the only way for some people to be able to accept that things are different now. It shows that I recognize my part in harming them. I am striving to leave the past behind and work towards a new future.

It is a good idea to touch base with a sponsor or trusted friend and rehearse amends. I did this with my sponsor when I reached certain people on my list. My sponsor gave me pointers on how to go about it and evaluated what I wanted to say. In this way I was lowering the risk of injuring them or myself. When I talk about injuring others, I mean that if I was able to make amends to a person and in doing so that person's life would be affected in a negative way, then I would want to rethink making direct amends.

My ex in-laws were the first people I was able to make amends to. I wrote each of my ex-husband's parents and siblings a letter. I was unable to make face to face amends because of the physical distance between us but was able to say everything I needed to in my letters. While I never heard back from my brother or sister in-law, my mother and father in-law eventually thawed to the point where we could communicate about their grandchildren. And once they realized I was not standing in the way of any relationship they might have with them, things improved considerably.

It was my actions that demonstrated my amends in this instance. Hopefully the rest of my in-law's family will come around as they see that actions have more meaning than excuses for past behaviors.

Some reactions were as expected. Some people had no clue why I was attempting to put things right. However, each amend lightened the baggage I had been carrying for years.

Questions:

What are the different ways to make amends to the people on your list?

Have you forgiven yourself and the person you have harmed before making the amends?

Are you expecting forgiveness from the person you are making amends to?

In what situation would indirect amends be more appropriate?

Activity

Pick out the hardest 3 or 4 amends you must make and rehearse them with a close friend or your sponsor. Note how you feel after practicing. Discuss the potential reactions you might encounter and how you might deal with them.

What is your motivation for making amends to a person on your list?

In what ways are you prepared for a negative reaction to your attempted amends?

Are you willing to let your Higher Power lead you in making amends?

Has making amends affected your relationships with others?

SLIP = Serenity/Sobriety Losing Its Priority

Have you received any feedback from those you have made amends to?

Give an example of how you are working step 9.

What are some of the topics of discussion have you and your sponsor/trusted friend have had in working this step?

Step 10

Continued to take personal inventory
and when we were wrong promptly admitted it.

This step is a daily working of steps four through nine. I try to find time every day to review my actions and interactions with others. Have I harmed anyone? Do I owe an amends? What do I need to work on? What have I done well? I have learned not to beat myself up when I do have a slip. I realize I am a work in progress.

I have found that if I ask my Higher Power every morning to help me get through the day, I have a better day. Then at night before I end the day, I conduct a personal inventory. My days seem to run smoother when I am actively working each of the steps. Step ten is considered a maintenance step. I use this step to keep my recovery on track, to stay healthy and to remember what I have learned so far.

If I have worked steps four through nine completely and honestly, I will have built a strong foundation and can continue on my journey of recovery.

I have noticed that when I am confronted with conflict, I am not reacting to it in the old manner. I am able to step back and reassess my response to the situation. When my ex-spouse is itching for a fight whether it be via email or over the phone, I know that I do not have to respond right away. I get to choose whether or not I pick up the phone or answer the email. React in my time, not theirs.

If I do over-react to a situation, I have learned to admit my mistake, apologize and move on. I don't stew over the problem, because the outcome was more than likely out of my control in the first place.

Questions:

Are you willing to take a personal inventory every day?

____

____

____

____

What kinds of things do you place on your personal inventory?

____

____

____

____

Do you look at your positive traits in your daily inventory?

____

____

____

____

How do you feel when you discover you are wrong?

____

____

____

____

An Attitude of Gratitude.

Why is it difficult for you to admit to others you were wrong?

Am I being kind and loving to all I come into contact?

In what ways do you involve your Higher Power in this step?

Do you continue to discuss your character defects/assets with your sponsor/trusted friend?

I would rather be happy than right.

Do you take a personal inventory every day and when you are wrong, promptly admit it? Why or why not?

Give an example of how you are working step 10.

What are some of the topics of discussion have you and your sponsor/trusted friend have had in working this step?

Step 11

Sought through prayer and meditation
to improve our conscious contact with God
as we understood Him,
praying only for knowledge of His will for us
and the power to carry that out

Learning how to be still is one way to keep serenity. I take time every day to listen to my Higher Power. Meditation clears my mind and keeps it open for new ideas. Concentrated breathing helps me through stressful events.

Step 11 keeps my focus on me. I can quit worrying about what everyone else is doing. Taking 10-15 minutes each day for myself can relax and rejuvenate me enough to make it through the day. Stopping each day and asking my Higher Power for direction in my life enables me to do the next right thing. Stopping, asking for help and listening for the answers gives me the ability to do my Higher Power's will. Tuning in is the only way I can figure out what God wants of me. I pray so that I have the strength to do what he asks.

One of the things I like about this step is that it allows me to choose who or what is my Higher Power. I started praying to my higher power long before I learned how to meditate. Meditation was hard for me. Sitting still for 10-15 minutes and trying to clear my mind was difficult. Stray thoughts would keep popping up and before I knew it I would be wrestling with a problem I had been thinking about earlier in the day.

Learning to focus on my breathing helped calm down my thoughts. I would either count my breaths up to five and start over or I would recite a mantra such as the Serenity Prayer over and over. Once I got the hang of meditating, I was able to focus on maintaining contact with my higher power and listen to what was needed of me in various situations.

It is my belief that this one step has caused me to stop and think about my response to situations that occur. It helps me think before I speak and/or react.

Questions:

Serenity is not the absence of turmoil but the ability to deal with it. How has working through the steps helped you deal with the turmoil in your life?

____

____

____

____

What is the difference between prayer and meditation?

____

____

____

____

____

____

____

____

How has prayer helped you? Meditation?

____

____

____

____

Keep in the solution, NOT the problem.

How can you take time out every day to pray and/or meditate?

How comfortable are you discussing your prayer and meditation practices with others?

What does conscious contact mean to you?

Do you to listen to your Higher Power and follow through on the directions you receive?

Stick with the winners!

What are some of the differences between Higher Power's will and your will?

____

____

____

____

How do you handle indecision?

____

____

____

____

Think about what you have been praying for...are your prayers entirely selfish or do you pray for others?

____

____

____

____

Have you sought through prayer and meditation to improve your conscious contact with your Higher Power and prayed for his will in your life and the power to carry it out?

____

Those who mind don't matter,

those who matter don't mind.

Give an example of how you are working step 11.

What are some of the topics of discussion have you and your sponsor/trusted friend have had in working this step?

Step 12

Having had a spiritual awakening as the result of these steps,
we tried to carry this message to others,
and to practice these principles in all our affairs.

Some spiritual awakenings happen over a period of time: some occur in a split second. Once it happened for me, I developed an urge to share my successes. In Al-anon this is called sharing Experience, Strength and Hope (ESH).

I discovered that I could use this program in other aspects of my life, (such as work) and not just in dealing with the alcoholic in my life. By practicing the principles I maintain serenity and peace. And if I have a slip, I know that I have a whole tool chest I can use to regain balance. These days my tool chest consists of reading literature, going to meetings, talking to my support group, applying a slogan and actively working the steps.

Actively working Step 12 every day is a goal of mine. My life has been changed by working these steps and I try to live my waking moments with these tools. My interactions with my friends and family have changed. I am in charge of my own life and am successful in taking care of my responsibilities.

I spend a lot of my time giving back to the community by speaking at a woman's shelter, writing this workbook and networking with recovery websites. I am dedicated to giving information about addiction and recovery.

I got well and now I can give back. These activities nurture the taking care of others aspect of my character and channel it in a good way. Seeking healthy relationships with others continue to be a challenge but with the completion of these 12 steps, I now know what to look for in my search.

Questions:

Describe your spiritual awakening.

How can you share your Experience, Strength and Hope with others?

In what ways can you demonstrate that the program works?

How does service work help in your recovery?

Life is like an onion;

you peel it one layer at a time;

and sometimes you cry.

Is sponsorship a role you would be willing to take on? Why or why not?

____

____

____

Define “these principles”.

____

____

____

____

Name some things that have changed about you since you have worked the steps.

____

____

____

____

What does “progress not perfection” mean to you?

____

____

____

____

I CAN’T do Higher Power’s will MY way.

Do you consider working the 12 steps to be a life-long program? Why?

Have you had a spiritual awakening as the result of these steps?

Can you describe your spiritual awakening?

Tried to carry this message to others?

How are you living the spiritual principles?

I've got some good news and some bad news for you:

The good news is that you're not in charge;

The bad news is that you're not in charge.

Give an example of how you are working step 12.

What are some of the topics of discussion you and your sponsor/trusted friend have had in working step 12?

SLOGANS

The following slogans are well known in 12 step programs. Which ones do you find the most helpful and why? Give an example of how you used each of these slogans in your recovery.

Easy Does It

How Important Is It?

Keep Coming Back

This Too Shall Pass

Let Go & Let God

Live and Let Live

One Day at a Time

It Works if you Work it

____

____

____

Progress not perfection.

____

____

____

My closing prayer:
I might wish you wealth,
or I might wish you health,
or that good fortune would caress you...
But wealth might bring sorrow,
good health could fail tomorrow,
so I'll simply say Higher Power Bless You!

Barbara Niemeyer

Other recovery books by AWS Media

Seeking Higher Power

www.amarjah.com

Made in the USA
Middletown, DE
24 March 2016